JUST
BREATHE

ILLUSTRATED BY MELISSA BAILEY

ANNETTE RIVLIN-GUTMAN

About the Author:

Annette Rivlin-Gutman is a passionate, award-winning writer and certified yoga instructor. A mother of two children, Annette drew upon her professional and personal experiences to write both of her children's books, *Mommy Has to Stay in Bed* and *Just Breathe*. She is also a former teacher and seasoned video producer with a strong background in educational and children's programming, including work with PBS, Mr. Rogers, and *Sesame Street*.

About the Illustrator:

Melissa Bailey has been drawing ever since she could hold a crayon. And now that she's a grownup, her childhood dream of being a children's book illustrator has come true! *Just Breathe* is the 32nd book she's had the privilege of illustrating. Melissa lives on a dirt road near a small town in Michigan, happily surrounded by family, friends, a poodle, and art supplies.

With gratitude and love for
Bruce, Anabelle, and Jory

It's the first day of school and I'm anxious to go.
Will I like my new teacher? Make new friends or a foe?

My mom says "Just breathe", so I deeply inhale.
I slowly breathe out, let my body set sail.

Instead of retreating, I trust how I feel.
I take a deep breath and my fear starts to heal.

I meet a new friend in my class during school.
We hang out together, I think he is cool.

Our feelings get hurt when we have a fight.
We both are upset, but I make it right.

I fill up my lungs, my breath full and deep.
I know that this friendship is something to keep.

I then can communicate, I then am aware,
and say that I'm sorry to show him I care.

Later that day, I take a math test.
I feel kind of worried, I feel kind of stressed.

How do I do it without wanting to cry?
Breathing deep through my nose helps keep my eyes dry.

Though tests make me shaky, one thing is for sure:
I know I can conquer any fears I endure.

The more that I'm challenged or things feel bleak,
I turn to my breath when it's calm that I seek.

After school, there is baseball, my first time to play.
Excited to try it, I waited all day.

Top of the fourth and I'm up at bat, nervous and scared, I keep fixing my hat.

"Remember, stay focused," I breathe in some air.
The ball flies right past, I swing at it with flair.

"Out!" yells the coach, disappointment and sighs.
Yet, I remain peaceful, what a surprise!

I may not have won or even touched base but I did do my best, I'm in a good space.

Hop in the car, you would think I'd be tired.
But, with all the excitement, my body is wired.

It's now time to sleep, yet I toss and I turn.
My thoughts in a jumble, too filled with concern.

Dad says, "Just breathe, make peace with the night."
Breathing quiets my mind and I'm out like a light.

I jump out of bed to face a new day.

Get ready for school and I'm on my way.

I breathe deeply to focus,
I breathe deeply and know,

I can take my breath with me wherever I go.

Made in the USA
San Bernardino, CA
18 July 2015